C000064672

ART POÉTIQUE

GUILLEVIC

ART POÉTIQUE

_____

TRANSLATED
by
MAUREEN SMITH

with
LUCIE ALBERTINI GUILLEVIC

BLACK
WIDOW
PRESS

BOSTON, MASS.

ART POETIQUE

Black Widow Press edition, April 2009.

Art Poétique © Editions GALLIMARD, Paris, 1989. This edition published by arrangement with Editions Gallimard. Special thanks to Florence Giry for her help with this edition and to Madame Lucie Albertini Guillevic.

English language translations and introduction © 2009 Maureen Smith.

cover photo: © Virginia Leiren.

All rights reserved. This book, or parts thereof, may not be reproduced in any form or by any means electronic, digital, or mechanical, including photocopy, scanning, recording, or any information storage and retrieval system now known or to be invented, without written permission from the publisher.

Black Widow Press is an imprint of Commonwealth Books, Inc., Boston.
Joseph S. Phillips, Publisher.
Distributed throughout North America/Canada/UK by NBN (National Book Network)

All Black Widow Press books are printed on acid-free paper.
Black Widow Press and its logo are registered trademarks of Commonwealth Books, Inc.

Black Widow Press
www.blackwidowpress.com

ISBN-13: 978-0-979-51376-3

Library of Congress Cataloging-in-Publication Data is available at the Library of Congress website: www.loc.gov

Prepress production by Windhaven Press (www.windhaven.com)

10 9 8 7 6 5 4 3 2 1

CONTENTS

INTRODUCTION

Guillevic's centred, precise, rigorous explorations in poetry, examining in detail every aspect of an experience, can be discerned in the originality and exactitude of his single-word titles: *Terraqué, Gagner, Sphère, Avec, Paroi, Présent, Maintenant, Relier,* etc. In *Paroi*, he enters into the difficulty of finding a way, of overcoming "something undefined / that taunts me, disturbs me." (*Paroi*, 186). *Art poétique* is not at all in the manner of earlier writers—Horace, Boileau, Verlaine, Mallarmé and others—in their various pronouncements about the poet's art. Guillevic's book is a highly personal account of the process and *experience* of writing poetry. One of the many distinctive features of his *Art poétique* is its extremely modest tone: it is not a doctrine or a series of rules about poetry, about what poetry is or should be, but the sharing of that profound experience, the personal research of a poet, his hesitations and doubts: "Do I see / What I see? / Do I hear / What I hear? Perhaps I see / What I hear, Perhaps I hear / What I see: Perhaps nothing/ Of all that, / A wisp of sounds, / Colours, forms." (*Art poétique*, 251).

Guillevic dedicates *Art poétique* to La Fontaine, whose mastery of the French language and fine sense of humour were an inspiration for him. From his early years he was a voracious reader, and many were the poets that he read and admired, in particular those whose virtuosity in the handling of the French language he considered to be outstanding, among them Villon, Racine, Baudelaire, Lamartine, Rimbaud and, later, Claudel. His social life was fired by contact with his contemporaries and their exchanges

1

about poetry and the poetic process. *Art poétique* was published in 1989, when, at the age of eighty-two, the poet had behind him a lifetime of reading and writing. His first collection, *Requiem*, appeared in 1938, when he was only thirty-one, and from then onwards there was a regular flow of poetic production, practically all of which is published by Gallimard. One might venture to say that much of his writing contains the seeds of *Art poétique*, for from the very beginning his obsession was poetry and the writing of poetry. Three books from the forties, *Terraqué* (1945), *Executoire* (1947) and *Gagner* (1949) end with poems whose title is "Art poétique":

> Words, words
> Don't allow themselves to be pushed around
> Like catafalques
>
> And all language
> Is foreign.   (*Terraqué*, 138)

Guillevic also recognised that *Inclus* (1973), was a kind of précis of the poet's art. Some sixteen years after its publication, the poet developed a further account of his experience in the present volume of 169 short poems, to which he gave the title of *Art poétique*. It begins with the words: "If I don't write this morning / I'll know no more about it." The key word in the opening poem is "know," for the acquisition of a form of knowledge through writing poetry was essential for him. Writing allowed him to know his surroundings, whether those of a Paris apartment, the plain of the Beauce around Chartres, or the Atlantic Ocean and the Breton coast and moors. It stimulated his attention to the physical universe and, at the same time, was a way to self-discovery. The contemplation of birds, insects, animals and plants gives rise to the eternal question directed to himself as poet, "What about you?"

> If the swallows
> Were not so skilful

> They would not fly
> As they fly,
>
> Would not direct
> Their flight with such boldness—
>
> What about you?   (*Art poétique*, 113)

But dialogue with the various aspects of the natural world is not enough. The poet has to enter into them, become them. "What does knowing mean?" he asks on contemplating the azure sky, "It's a matter of living in it / Feeling oneself in it, / Feeling one is the blue sky." (*Maintenant*, 43). Knowledge is entry into the very being of things: "Things of the earth, / Of the sky, the ocean, / I want to live with you, / I want to be you." (*Maintenant*, 28). To know, to live, to be, to become; the verbal progression describes the movement that leads to this intimate form of knowledge:

> To be
> Where and what?
>
> No matter where,
> But not only in oneself.
>
> To be in the world.
> A fragment, an element of the world.
>
> Superior to nothing,
> To nobody, not even to the falling rain.
>
> To feel equal
> And the same as the dandelion, the slug,

Inferior to nothing,
Neither to the baobab, nor to the horizon,

To live with everything
That's outside and inside,

Everything that is the world's,
In the world.

Wisp of straw, no!
Cathedral, no!

A breath of life
Trying to last.   (*Art poétique*, 349)

Being, feeling, living, trying to last like every other element of the universe, Guillevic emphasises in this poem his sense of *égalité* with all things. In *Le Chant* he develops the notion that they all, like the poet, have their own song. This song, which is the song of the world, can only be learned in the silence of the world:

The white page
Only succeeds in singing

Through the silence
Imposed upon it.   (*Le Chant*, 399)

*

The most
Silent singing

Is not the song

Of silence.

It's the song
Of the night seeking itself out.   (*Le Chant*, 391)

"Sculpting silence at the edge of night" (*Avec,* 45), Guillevic is essentially and principally the poet of silence, convinced of the power of the drift of silence, a silence that is "everywhere, for it has no source." (*Inclus*, 123). This silence is to be found especially within himself, in his own depths. On hearing the drone of a tractor accompanying the silence of the fields, he writes: "All the work is done / Underground and on the earth / By the grass, the roots." (*Avec,* 161). This deep and essential need for silence has a cleansing effect: "It's as if / Diving deep into silence / Washed me, purified me." (*Du silence,* 180). The poet expresses his delight that silence exists, and exists within himself, where silence and joy are inseparable. (*Possibles futurs,* 179). The poet, who "places silence above all things," the "one who entrusts / his joy to silence" (*Le Chant,* 163) is the only one who can ponder the value of song. Like music, poetry has its origins in these zones of silence, the calm places of ecstasy and joy where the real that one knows and the process of invention can meet. Silence must be allowed to take its course: "Let silence do its work / Let it do as it pleases." (*Maintenant*, 45). The poet is "Forever seeking / The sources of silence", (*Maintenant*, 46), only to find that the poem itself leads to further depths of silence:

Like some music
The poem makes silence sing,

Leads us until we touch
Another silence,

Even more silence.   (*Art poétique*, 75)

Many poets have written poems about the art of writing poetry; few have

written with such conviction of the need for silence, and of the complemen-
tarity of silence and word, of silence and music, of silence and the song of
the world. For the poet, silence is a requisite of intense inner attention. It
precedes a vital search for emptiness, "letting go" all that might impede the
flow of language. "Make within myself that emptiness" is his aesthetic aim
on his quest for poetry. Silence penetrates the states of consciousness that
precede expression.

 Art poétique records an enduring experience of silence and the culmina-
tion of a great passion. Each poem is of a rare intensity. The need to write
flows from Guillevic's own need, but it also comes from elsewhere. Rarely
does he use the word "inspiration," but often the word "*souffle*," breath.
There is as it were a triple source for poetry: first, the "*souffle*" coming
from elsewhere, second, the consciousness of his own roots, his capacity
to live "among the roots" and be a "root-dweller," and third the realisa-
tion that language is derived from time past, an inheritance from our ances-
tors, for they prepared, they "chewed" the words we use today. (*Inclus*, 20).
For Guillevic, the poet is the one who "knots together earth and word."
(*Inclus*, 94). The action of digging deep into the soil of language is a constant image. Guillevic delves into the earth, and declares: "I will go deep /
Into my labyrinths" (*Inclus*, 159-60):

> Enclose yourself within yourself
> As tightly as you can.
>
> Then you'll be in touch
> With the deep zones
>
> Of you know not what.   (*Maintenant*, 110)

 This "you know not what" is the source of the mystery that poetry holds:
"Whatever you do / The poem holds mystery." (*Art poétique*, 297). This
mystery is the mystery of poetry and also the mystery of the universe: its

shellfish, its precious or semi-precious stones, its rocks and molluscs, its bird life and plant forms. Earth and cosmos constitute Guillevic's universe. His images of verticality extend from deep in the earth to the highest point in the cosmos, and he enters into both. His need for cosmic space entices him to find a centre within this space, for the act of writing will only take place in the centre, within "a place resembling a cave." (*Inclus*, 120). And the descent into the cave, with its silence, is a genuine need:

> I would like
> To speak silence.
>
> Silence
> Speaks of the centre.
>
> They are
> What I need. (*Art poétique,* 159)

The poet's calling is "To write, / To inscribe, / To mark, / To engrave, / To delve, / To keep, / Not just anywhere, / Not even / In stone / In wood / Only / In space, / In the centre."(*Inclus*, 52).

What is this space, this centre? Is it concrete or abstract, is it real space or dream-space? Guillevic's universe is all of this. The poet occupies, or expresses the desire to occupy, the very centre of this space, into which there filters a dream background coexisting with the memory of the diverse natural elements of his native Brittany, which in some way enter into almost the entirety of his poetic production. "Let me go deep / into my imaginary / yet real sea." (*Art poétique,* 201). The ocean, the sea-winds, the granite rocks and the clouds inhabit permanently his poetic space and become both dream-space and concrete space, the materiality of a world experienced and the private zone of a world remembered. It is through penetration into this harmonious co-existence, this personal domain, and into the life and substance of the words which convey it, that the poet is able to be in touch with both materiality and memory. Within his verbal and visual space, his space of silence, the solidity of his universe remains erect and expectant, like the stonecarver's block of marble or the carpenter's supply of timber, to be prepared, chiselled, planed, formed into a construct that will "hold."

For Guillevic the word "hold", *tenir,* is essential. Each composition, each poem, must "hold", remain firm, well-balanced, and endure. All the various elements which inhabit his universe are also markers in a world in which it is so easy to lose one's way. "Only the poet," wrote William Carlos Williams in a letter to Denise Levertov, "has not lost his way." Guillevic is not lost. He is at home in a world which for many years he found alienating, a world which excluded him, but in which he persevered in a spirit of solidarity with people and things:

> . . . I speak of all that is
> In the name of all that has form and is formless.
>
> All that has weight
> All that is weightless . . .   (*Gagner*, 183)

He created his own world which he refers to as a "domain", a "kingdom" or a "sphere", the place where something new is expected to come into existence, and in which he searches for a language of concreteness and clarity: "I don't like / There to be within me // Any kind of fog / Encroaching on my domain// Not letting me see / Where I am, where I'm up to. // So I attack, I collect / Everything I find inside //And everything I root up outside / In aid of clarity or a means to bring it to birth. // In that outside, / The words pierce through.// Words are swords / To the bellies of the fogs." (*Art poétique***,** 57). In this domain, the search for language entails an experience of fullness and void, darkness and light, silence and singing. Sensitive, like his contemporary the painter Camille Bryen, to the existence of void and fullness, Guillevic recognises their presence "even in silence."(*Inclus*, 132). It is this void that allows entry, allows the perception of the murmur at the heart of the void (*Inclus,* 135). Guillevic is constantly

in quest of the sacred in the ordinary: each hour, each day resplendent with
the sacred:

> I dream of a society that would be steeped in the sacred. In my
> view, the poet should help others to live the sacred in everyday
> life. The sacred, that sentiment that exalts you, forces your
> respect, puts you in touch with something that magnifies you and
> can destroy you. The risk of total joy.   (*Living in Poetry*, 113)

The passion of writing, expressed in terms of the natural world, of space
and curve, of becoming, and indeed of sacrifice, is not an experience of
darkness, for joy cohabits with the sacrificial pain, the "joy-filled difficulty"
of writing. What does this "sacrifice" consist of? It is the yielding up of the
self, the giving of one's innermost experience, into the birthing process of
the poem. For each poem is " . . . the first adventure / The last, the only
one / Where everything is in play / Everything is given." (*Art poétique*,
187). For Guillevic, who spoke of himself as a "prehistoric" man, poetry
should go back to origins. The task of the poet is to transform given language: "To write / is to find another use / for the language of the land. /
Something else. For example, / To make wire / Out of string . . . " Poets
are makers, and from the flexibility and suppleness of words (string), poetry
is wrought through the creation of rhythm and tension (wire) in the lines
they make. The "everything" of language, Guillevic tells us, "comes from
elsewhere." (*Inclus*, 54).

Guillevic's overall practice was to develop a notion or a theme through
a series of short poems, considering the subject from different viewpoints,
with its different facets. In *Inclus* and *Art poétique* he contemplates the
poet's art from a variety of angles. In *Paroi* his approach is similar, looking
at a situation from every possible point of view. His practice in *The Singing* is also to study every aspect of the song of the world. One is tempted
to draw a comparison between this approach and that of Cézanne, for
Guillevic's discovery of Cézanne was of some importance in his awareness
of his own art. Cézanne's *motifs* come to mind immediately, for Guillevic

has a collection of poems with that very title. More particularly, Cézanne's use of the multiple facet allows us to visualise a single reality from various standpoints. And what we call in Hopkins' terms *inscape*—"the distinctive form of natural objects"—and *instress*—the energy of being by which things are upheld, and the natural stress which determines an inscape, can also shed light on Guillevic's art. For Hopkins, the meaning of the word inscape was many-faceted, as we can see from his notebooks. Guillevic showed constant interest in the form, characteristics and inner life of things and in their total integrity. This integrity is revealed through the strict laws and discipline of inscape, requiring the most intense attentiveness. He perceived objects in their particular inscape and in relationship to the poet and to one another.

Numerous books, theses and articles about Guillevic have been published in universities and by poets and critics throughout the world. The appeal of this writer is immense, and appears to be increasing, if one takes into account the conferences, publications, readings, exhibitions and other events organised over the past few years since his death in 1997. His early life in Brittany, his youth in Alsace, his adult life in Paris as a senior civil servant *Inspecteur de l'économie*, and his travels all over the globe brought him into contact with language and languages, people and peoples, ways of thinking and ways of being. There is an openness about his poetry which is attractive to today's reader. In spite of his very solid grounding in earlier forms of poetry, his short poems, which he liked to call *quanta,* are very modern in their simplicity and directness.

Guillevic was open to other contemporary art forms, and his poems have been an inspiration for a large number of artists, many among them the best-known artists of his time, such as Dubuffet, Léger, Manessier and Bazaine, with whom the poet was happy to collaborate. Some 140 artists' books exist, and they are the proof of the wide diversity of style and genre of these artists attracted by his work. More recently, we have been able to appreciate the work of Jean Cortot, Bertrand Dorny, Thierry Le Saëc, Loïc le Groumellec, Marie Alloy and many others. Guillevic's poetry has also inspired the work of musicians, among them André Bon, Michel Puig,

François Rossé, Isabelle Aboulker, Pierre-Yves Level, Lothar Voigtländer, Jacques Demière, Thierry Machuel.

Readers of English may be familiar with earlier translations of Guillevic: that of Denise Levertov published by New Directions in New York in 1968, that of Teo Savory, Unicorn Press, Santa Barbara, 1968, and her translation of *Selected Poems* in the Penguin Modern Poets series in 1974, and John Montague's translation of *Carnac* published by Bloodaxe in 1999. I translated the 1980 interviews by Lucie Albertini and Alain Vircondelet, *Vivre en poésie / Living in Poetry* which were published by the Dedalus Press in Dublin in 1999. More recently, in 2007, Black Widow Press in Boston published Patricia Terry's anthology of Guillevic's poems under the title of *The Sea and Other Poems.* Guillevic's poems have been translated into more than fifty other languages, languages as different as German, Spanish, Korean, Chinese and Icelandic. *Art poétique* was translated into Spanish in 2005.

The present translation of *Art poétique* was undertaken in close collaboration with Lucie Albertini Guillevic, whose intimate knowledge of her husband's poems and her lifetime experience of the translation of contemporary poetry from several countries, has been of vital importance in the search for clarity and fidelity in the translation of the original text. In spite of current practice in a great deal of poetry in English, we have retained the use of capital letters at the beginning of each line, thus respecting Guillevic's way of writing, the visual impact of his poems and the very slight variation of pace which such a practice entails. We have also been careful to respect his liking for the word *azur*, which became increasingly frequent in his later work. We have translated it to the English "azure," in the understanding that in Guillevic's use of the word there was an oblique reference to Mallarmé. Guillevic's preference for the word is clearly defined in a poem in *Art poétique,* in which he declares that in spite of "wear and tear", and it's being "one of those terms called poetic",/ I use / The word azure, I write it, // For it expresses / The blue sky, of a blue // Inviolate/ Even by the firmament."A further difficulty was in the translation of the word "*armoire,*" in Guillevic's work an pervasive death/life image. The various possibilities in English—cupboard, closet, press, etc.—do not convey adequately the image of the Breton solid oak *armoire*, which after consideration we left in the original French. Sometimes Guillevic used terms taken from the world of science, and in *Art poétique* we have come across a term from modern mathematics, "an empty set," which, had we translated literally would have involved a loss of meaning. Such difficulties, however, are but slight when compared with the pleasure and privilege of entering into the poet's universe through the many hours of work and research that translation of poetry requires.

Special thanks are due to Patricia Terry for reading the manuscript and for suggestions made, and to Catherine Boylan, Moya Cannon and Monique Chefdor.

In the shortest poem in *Art poétique*, Guillevic gives this brief and eloquent résumé of his experience of writing:

> The poem
> Brings us into the world.   (*Art poétique*, 301)

Maureen Smith
Paris, March 19, 2008.

For Jean de La Fontaine

Si je n'écris pas ce matin,
Je n'en saurai pas davantage,

Je ne saurai rien
De ce que je peux être.

If I don't write this morning
I'll know no more about it,

I'll know nothing
Of what I can be.

Si j'écris, c'est disons
Pour ouvrir une porte.

Le plus curieux
J'ignore

À quel moment se fait
Cette ouverture.

D'ailleurs, ce qui se lève
C'est peut-être un rideau.

If I write, let's say
It's to open a door.

Strange:
I don't know

Just when this opening
Takes place.

—Besides, it's perhaps
A curtain that's raised.

Quand j'écris,
C'est comme si les choses,

Toutes, pas seulement
Celles dont j'écris,

Venaient vers moi
Et l'on dirait et je crois

Que c'est
Pour se connaître.

When I write,
It's as if things,

All of them, not only
Those I write about,

Came towards me
And it would seem and I believe

That it's
To get acquainted.

Lorsque j'écris nuage,
Le mot nuage,

C'est qu'il se passe quelque chose
Avec le nuage,

Qu'entre nous deux
Se tisse un lien,

Que pour nous réunir
Il y a une histoire,

Et quand l'histoire est finie
Le roman s'écrit dans le poème.

When I write cloud,
The word cloud,

Something happens
With the cloud,

And between the two of us
A bond is made,

To bring us together
There's a story,

And when the story's over
The novel is written in the poem.

Voici une chenille,
Elle rampe.

Elle rampe vers de la nourriture.
C'est du moins ce qu'elle croit,

Et d'ailleurs c'est vrai,
Mais aussi elle rampe

Vers son avatar,
Vers sa vie de papillon,

Et cet objectif
Elle ne le devine pas.

-Toi, tu ne devines pas encore
Vers quoi tu écris.

Here's a caterpillar.
It's climbing.

It's climbing towards some food.
At least that's what it thinks,

Moreover it's true,
But it's also climbing

Towards its avatar,
Towards its butterfly life,

And can't figure out
This aim.

—You still haven't figured out
Towards what you are writing.

Apparemment,
Tu ne fais pas de gestes.

Tu es assis là sans bouger,
Tu regardes n'importe quoi,

Mais en toi
Il y a des mouvements qui tendent

Dans une espèce de sphère
À saisir, à pénétrer,

À donner corps
À je ne sais quels flottements

Qui peu à peu deviennent des mots,
Des bouts de phrase,

Un rythme s'y met
Et tu acquiers un bien.

Apparently,
You make no gestures.

You sit there without moving,
Looking at any old thing,

But within you
There are movements that stretch

Within a kind of sphere
To grasp, to penetrate,

To embody
Who knows what wavering

Which little by little becomes words,
Bits of sentences,

A rhythm intervenes
And you acquire an asset.

Dans la plaine,
Un arbre
Se détache sur le ciel.

Heureusement,
Car je m'y accroche.

Je le constate et je me demande
Si plutôt qu'à l'arbre
Ce n'est pas au mot que je m'accroche,

Par exemple, ici,
Au mot noyer qui le designe.

On the plain
A tree
Stands out against the sky.

It's a good thing,
For I hang on to it.

I realize this and wonder
Whether it's the word I hang on to
Rather than the tree,

For example, in this case,
The word "walnut tree" that refers to it.

J'ai l'habitude
De me considérer

Comme vivant avec des racines,
Principalement celles des chênes.

Comme elles
Je creuse dans le noir

Et j'en ramène de quoi
Offrir du travail

À la lumière.

I have the habit
Of considering myself

A root-dweller,
Mainly among those of oaks.

Like them
I delve in the dark

And bring back something
To give work

To the light.

Aujourd'hui,
C'est le jour du soleil.

Il n'est pas triomphal,
Il n'est pas solennel,
Il est content d'être soleil.

Toutes les choses
Se plaisent à la définition
Qu'elles se donnent.

C'est le jour
Où le soleil écrit son poème.

Today
Is the day of the sun.

It's not exultant,
It's not solemn,
It's content to be sun.

All things
Take pleasure in the definition
They give themselves.

It's the day
When the sun writes its poem.

Mon poème et la cathédrale :
Quelque parenté.

Ils sont debout,
Tendant leur pointe

À la verticale,
Vers le haut,

Accueillant qui vient
Apporter son soi-même,

S'essayer à grandir.

My poem and the cathedral:
Some kind of kinship.

They stand
Pointing their tops

Vertically,
Skywards,

Welcoming whoever comes
Bringing his own self,

Trying to grow.

Le chant
Peut être silence.

Le silence peut exister
Pour qui chante,

Pour lui
Et pour tous,

Car il porte le chant
À travers les horizons.

Singing
Can be silence.

Silence can exist
For whoever is singing,

For him
And for everyone,

For he carries the song
Across the horizons.

Je n'aime pas le mystère,
Je le hais.

Je ne le fuis pas
Mais je le cherche
Pour le cerner,

Pour délivrer les lieux
Qui ne sont pas à lui.

Je le hais peut-être
De trop bien le sentir
À défaut d'y entrer.

Ce mystère que je cerne,
Il colle à mon mystère.

Ils font à tous les deux
Un ensemble sans vide

Et j'ai besoin de vide
Où le mystère que je dis mien
Puisse flotter à sa guise.

I don't like mystery,
I hate it.

I don't run away from it
But I seek it out
So as to encompass it,

To liberate the places
Not its own.

Perhaps I hate it
Because I feel it too much
For want of entering into it.

The mystery I encompass
Clings to my mystery.

One with the other they make
Some kind of fullness

And I need emptiness
Where the mystery I call mine
Can enjoy floating.

Je suis comme l'eau
Qui doit obéir.

Je suis comme les nuages
Qui doivent aller
Et tomber en pluie.

I'm like water
That has to obey.

I'm like clouds
That have to go
And fall as rain.

Tu voudrais bien
Avancer dans ton poème
Comme un ruisseau

Sinueux, pas rapide—

Et tu trembles de devenir
Comme un étang

Où tu pourrais, stagnant,
Ne plus t'y reconnaître.

You'd like
To advance in your poem
Like a stream

Sinuous, not swift—

And you tremble in awe
Of becoming like a pond

Where,stagnant, you might no longer
Recognize yourself.

Il n'y a pas dans ce monde
Que des étangs.

Pourquoi les voir,
Les chercher partout,
Y penser tellement ?

À quoi ça sert
D'avoir tant écrit sur eux ?

Et sans savoir pourquoi.

Ponds are not
The only thing in this world.

Why see them,
Look for them everywhere
Give them so much thought?

What's the use
Of having written so much about them?

And without knowing why.

Toi,
Tu regardes le corbeau,

Tu t'intéresses à ce qu'il fait
Sur les chaumes
Devant ta fenêtre.

Lui,
Rien ne l'oblige,
Il ne te regarde pas écrire.

You
Look at the crow,

You're interested in what it's doing
On the thatch
Outside your window.

It
Has no obligation,
It doesn't watch you writing.

Je suis comme le lierre :
J'aime grimper,

Mais je n'ai pas
De tronc, de mur où me coller.

Pourtant il me faut grimper.
Alors, que faire ?

Je grimpe,
Même si ce n'est qu'en moi

I'm like the ivy:
I like to climb.

But I have
No trunk or wall to cling to.

But I need to climb.
So what shall I do?

I climb,
If only within myself.

Ce n'est pas facile
D'être un mur,

Tout seul
Entre deux propriétés.

De temps en temps,
Le vent, un oiseau.

Le mur ne peut écrire
Qu'au ciel, au tilleul,

Mais il sait, lui,
Qu'il écrit en incluant sa base.

It's not easy
To be a wall,

Alone
Between two properties.

From time to time,
The wind, a bird.

The wall can only write
To the sky, to the lime tree,

But it knows that what it writes
Involves its foundation.

On n'en finit jamais
Avec la lune.

On a beau la regarder,
La peindre, écrire sur elle,

Lui parler,
Essayer de la caresser,

Lui tourner le dos,
L'insulter,

Quand elle est là
Elle nous verse son lait,

Quand elle n'y est pas,
Son lait nous manque.

We've never seen the last
Of the moon.

We can look at it,
Paint it, write about it,

Talk to it,
Try to stroke it,

Turn our back on it,
Insult it,

When it's there
It pours out its milk,

When it's not there,
We miss its milk.

Qu'est-ce qu'il t'arrive ?

Il t'arrive des mots,
Des lambeaux de phrase.

Laisse-toi causer. Ecoute-toi
Et fouille, va plus profond.

Regarde au verso des mots,
Démêle cet écheveau.

Rêve à travers toi,
À travers tes années
Vécues et à vivre.

What's the matter with you?

The matter with me is words,
Fragments of sentences.

Let yourself ramble on. Listen to yourself
And excavate, dig deeper.

Look at the back of words.
Untangle that hank.

Dream your own dreams
Across the years
Lived and to be lived.

Et l'hirondelle ?

Elle va, vient, tourne, revient,
Bec ouvert sans doute,
À la recherche de sa proie,

Crie parfois,
Se repose peu.

Le pigeon s'agite moins,
Reste souvent immobile sur une branche,

Attendant que monte en lui
Le recoulement.

And the swallow?

It comes and goes, turns, returns,
Open-beaked no doubt,
Looking for prey,

Twitters at times,
Rests but little.

The pigeon less flustered
Often stays still on a branch,

Waiting for the cooing
To rise within it.

Je n'aime pas
Qu'il y ait en moi

Ces espèces de brouillards
Qui empiètent sur mon domaine

Et ne me laissent pas voir
Où je suis, où j'en suis.

Alors, j'attaque, je ramasse
Tout ce qu'au dedans je trouve

Et tout ce qu'au dehors j'arrache
Comme clarté ou moyen d'en faire naître.

Dans ce dehors,
Les mots percent.

Les mots sont des épées
Contre les ventres des brouillards.

I don't like
There to be within me

Any kind of fog
Encroaching on my domain

Not letting me see
Where I am, where I'm up to.

So I attack, I collect
Everything I find inside

And everything I uproot outside
In aid of clarity or a means to bring it to birth.

In that outside,
The words pierce through.

Words are swords
To the bellies of the fogs.

Je ne sais pas comment
Marcher sur les nuages.

Alors je l'imagine
Et ça dure.

Surtout
Si je ne regarde pas

Et rêve
À ce que je vais écrire.

I don't know
How to walk on clouds.

So I imagine it
And it lasts,

Especially
If I don't look

And dream
Of what I'm going to write.

Il te faut de la pauvreté
Dans ton domaine.

C'est comme ce besoin qu'on peut avoir
D'un mur blanchi à la chaux.

Une richesse, une profusion
De mots, de phrases, d'idées

T'empêcheraient de te centrer,
D'aller, de rester

Là où tu veux,
Où tu dois aller

Pour ouvrir,
Pour recueillir.

Ta chambre intérieure
Est un lieu de pauvreté.

You need some poverty
In your domain.

It's like the need you can feel
For a whitewashed wall.

A wealth, a profusion
Of words, sentences, ideas

Would not let you be centred,
Or go, or stay

Wherever you want,
Wherever you have to go

To open up,
To remain in silence.

Your inner chamber
Is a place of poverty.

Enchanter d'autres que toi
Peut les aider

À se mettre
Pour changer le monde

Dans le sens
Que dit le chant

Vers la hauteur qu'il annonce,
Vers l'horizon qu'il montre,

Un horizon
Au plus fort de la possession
De lui-même par lui.

Enchanting other people
Can help them

To get started
On changing the world

The way
The song goes

Towards the heights it announces,
Towards the horizon it points to,

A horizon
In its utmost
Self-possession.

Ce que je crois ne pas savoir,
Ce que je n'ai pas en mémoire,

C'est le plus souvent,
Ce que j'écris dans mes poèmes.

What I think I don't know,
What I don't remember

Is most often
What I write in my poems.

Tu n'en finiras donc jamais ?

Encore un poème,
Encore un,

Cette pensée t'agace
Et même elle t'affole.

Ce besoin d'infini
Qui fait bouger la mer.

Mais si une fois
Tu t'arrêtais pour de bon,

Tu serais un creux
Comme entre deux vagues.

Will you never finish?

Another poem;
Still another,

This thought irritates you
And even throws you into turmoil.

This need for the infinite
That makes the sea move.

But if ever
You stopped yourself for good,

You would be a trough
As it were between two waves.

Irons-nous plus loin ?
Irons-nous plus
Au cœur des choses ?

La où tu dirais : c'est bien.
Là où il n'y aurait
Que complicité,

Comme un besoin
De donner à tout
Sa bénédiction,

Là où atteindre enfin
La cinquième dimension,

Là où le fleuve angoisse
Finit dans l'océan.

Shall we go further?
Shall we go deeper
Into the heart of things?

Wherever you say: it's all right.
Wherever there would be
Only complicity,

Like a need
To give everything
One's blessing,

Where the fifth dimension
Can finally be reached,

Where the river anguish
Ends up in the ocean.

Il n'aura pas,
Mon poème,
La force des explosifs.

Il aidera chacun
À se sentir vivre
À son niveau de fleur en travail,

À se voir
Comme il voit la fleur.

My poem
Will not have
The force of explosives.

It will help everyone
On their own level
To feel like a flower at work

To see themselves
As they see the flower.

À ras de terre
Chanter mon solo

Comme le pissenlit
Que je voudrais être

Au fond du jardin.

Close to the ground
To sing my solo

Like the dandelion
I would like to be

At the end of the garden.

Comme certaines musiques
Le poème fait chanter le silence,

Amène jusqu'à toucher
Un autre silence,

Encore plus silence.

Like some music
The poem makes silence sing,

Leads us until we touch
Another silence,

Even more silence.

Dans le poème
On peut lire

Le monde comme il apparaît
Au premier regard.

Mais le poème
Est un miroir

Qui offre d'entrer
Dans le reflet

Pour le travailler,
Le modifier.

—Alors le reflet modifié
Réagit sur l'objet
Qui s'est laissé refléter.

In the poem
You can read

The world as it appears
At first glance.

But the poem
Is a mirror

That invites us to enter
The reflection

So as to mould it,
Modify it.

—Then the modified reflection,
Affects the object
That has let itself be reflected.

Avec la lune,
Avec la lande,

Jouer à : je suis,
Je ne suis pas
Ton miroir.

With the moon,
With the moors,

Play at: I am,
I am not
Your mirror.

Chaque poème

A sa dose d'ombre,
De refus.

Pourtant, le poème
Est tourné vers l'ouvert

Et sous l'ombre qu'il occupe
Un soleil perce et rayonne.

Un soleil qui règne.

Every poem

Has its portion of shadow,
Of refusal.

But the poem
Is turned toward the open

And beneath the shadow it occupies
A sun pierces through and shines.

A sun that rules.

Tout n'est pas chute,

Descente à l'infini,
Plus ou moins.

À preuve, la montée
Avec le poème,
Dans le poème.

Not everything plummets

Descends to infinity,
More or less.

For proof, the ascent
With the poem,
In the poem.

Dans ton poème
Il y a le coucou.

Tu as souvent
Parlé de lui.

Alors souvenons-nous,
Vivons avec lui

Un printemps qui traverse
Toutes les saisons.

In your poem
There's the cuckoo.

You have often
Talked about it,

So let's remember,
Let's live with it

A spring that crosses
All seasons.

Tu ne feras pas l'éloge.

Louanger, c'est t'écarter,
Te séparer
De ce que tu louanges.

Car on ne louange pas du dedans,
Mais assurément du dehors.

Tu te tairas, parleras
Avec une chose
Ou avec son absence,

Tu la cajoleras,
Te feras cajoler par elle.

Même le nuage
N'a pas pouvoir
De refuser la caresse.

You'll not sing praises.

To praise, is to drift away,
To separate yourself
From what you praise.

For one does not praise from within,
But certainly from without.

You'll be quiet, you'll speak
With a thing
Or with its absence,

You'll cajole it,
You'll let yourself be cajoled by it.

Even the cloud
Has no power
To refuse the caress.

Il y a de l'utopie
Dans le brin d'herbe

Et sans cela
Il ne pousserait pas.

Il y a de l'utopie
Dans l'azur

Et même
Dans un ciel gris.

Toi, sans utopie
Tu n'écrirais pas

Puisqu'en écrivant
Ce que tu cherches

C'est mieux connaître
Où te mène ton utopie.

There's utopia
In the blade of grass

And without that
It wouldn't grow.

There's utopia
In the azure sky

And even
In a grey sky.

Without utopia
You wouldn't write

Because in writing,
What you're looking for

Is to better understand
Where your own utopia is leading you.

Mon poème n'est pas
Chose qui s'envole
Et fend l'air.
Il ne revient pas de la nue.

C'est tout juste si parfois
Il plane un court moment
Avant d'aller rejoindre
La profondeur terrestre.

My poem is not
A thing that flies away
And cleaves the air.
It doesn't drop from the skies.

It almost seems
To hover for a while
Before it returns
To the depths of the earth.

Mon poème

Parle du tréfonds
De la terre qu'il veut.

Il décèle comment
La terre se tasse

Pour se rassurer.

My poem

Speaks of the depths
Of the earth that it wants.

It discovers how
The earth settles

To reassure itself.

Ne comptez pas sur moi
Pour en dire plus
Que ce que j'ai vécu
Ou voulu vivre.

Chaque poème
Est une aventure
En même temps
Que le constat de l'aventure.

Pas plus—
Sauf le désir
D'aller plus
Dans l'aventure

Et le besoin
D'inventer ce plus
En l'écrivant
Au corps-à-corps.

Don't count on me
To say any more
Than what I have lived
Or wanted to live

Each poem
Is an adventure
At the same time
As the report of the adventure.

Nothing more—
Except the desire
To go further
Into the adventure

And the need
To invent this more
By writing it
In a tussle.

Le cercle
Est la meilleure figure
Pour le poème.

Curieux :
Lorsque je dis cercle
Je vois une lande

Et je cherche à deviner
Ce qu'il peut y avoir
Au milieu.

Je ne bouge pas,
Me laisse faire
Par cette lande,

Ce cercle imaginaire
Qui a pris corps.

The circle
Is the best shape
For the poem.

Strange:
When I say circle
I see a moor

And I try to guess
What there might be
In the middle.

I don't move,
I abandon myself
To this moor,

This imaginary circle
Embodied.

J'écris pour la gloire,
J'écris aussi pour la gloire.

Pas pour celle qu'on donne,
Pour celle que je me donne.

La gloire de me dire :
J'ai fait un poème,

J'ai, comme dit Hölderlin,
Réussi le poème.

I write for glory,
I also write for the glory,

Not for the kind they give,
For the kind I give myself.

The glory of saying to myself :
I've made a poem,

I have, as Hölderlin says,
Been successful with the poem.

Quand un poème t'arrive,
Tu ne sais d'où ni pourquoi,

C'est comme si un oiseau
Venait se poser dans ta main,

Et tu te penches,
Tu te réchauffes à son corps.

On peut aussi partir
À la recherche de l'oiseau.

When a poem comes to you,
You know not whence or why,

It's as if a bird
Came and perched on your hand,

And you bend over,
Warming yourself with its body.

You can also go out
In search of the bird.

Il y a un trou
Dans le nuage
Qui occupe le ciel

Et cela me donne
Encore plus envie
D'écrire le poème
Qui cherche à travers moi.

There's a gap
In the cloud
Dwelling in the sky

And that makes me
Want even more
To write the poem
On its quest through me.

Le soleil couchant
Peut avoir des couleurs

Qui font croire
Qu'il est plus qu'un soleil mort.

Rien de pareil
Pour le poème.

Il crie toujours :
Je vis, prenez-moi.

Et, sachez-le,
Je ne me suiciderai pas.

Je suis un trou dans le réseau
Que constitue partout la mort.

The setting sun
Can have colours

That make you believe
It's only a dead sun.

Nothing like that
For the poem.

It always shouts :
I'm alive, take me.

And look,
I'll not commit suicide,

I'm a hole in the network
That death sets up everywhere.

Je regarde et je vois.

Tout à coup
Quelque chose se passe

Qui s'attaque
À ce que je vois,

L'éloigne et l'approche,
L'enfonce et l'élève.

Je touche sans toucher,
On me frôle sans m'approcher.

I look and I see.

Suddenly
Something happens

Attacking
What I can see,

Keeping it at a distance and drawing it near,
Pushing it down and raising it up.

I touch without touching,
Am jostled and not approached.

Je suis ici.
Je ne fais rien.

Mais peut-être
Suis-je à la chasse.

I'm here.
Doing nothing.

But maybe
I'm out hunting.

Ce n'est pas une raison
Pour te soustraire
À ce qui se passe dans le monde.

Tu ne le pourrais pas.

Tous ces événements
S'insinuent dans ces noirs
Qui sont en toi et pèsent.

Ils se collent à ce que tu vois,
Aux rues, aux paysages,

Ils colorent et remuent
Ces choses
Que tu regardes.

L'humus toujours te parle
De massacres.

It's not a reason
To evade
What's happening in the world.

You couldn't.

All these events
Work their way into the dark places
That are inside you and weigh heavy.

They cling to what you see,
The streets, the landscapes.

They tinge and they disturb
These things
You look at.

Humus always speaks to you
Of massacres.

Si les hirondelles
N'étaient pas si savantes,

Elles ne voleraient pas
Comme elles volent.

Ne dirigeraient pas
Leur vol avec cette hardiesse -

Mais toi ?

If the swallows
Were not so skilful,

They wouldn't fly
As they fly,

Wouldn't direct
Their flight with such boldness -

What about you?

L'hirondelle
Et la grenouille.

À toi de trouver pourquoi
Elles apparaissent en toi
Au même instant.

À toi de trouver
Ce qu'elles partagent

Dans ce réseau où tu patauges
Avec le ciel, avec la mare

Et cette espèce de lumière
Que tu aimes voir venir
Te rapprocher des choses.

The swallow
And the frog.

It's up to you to find out why
They appear in you
At the same instant.

It's up to you to find out
In this network where you flounder

What they have in common
With the sky, with the pond

And this kind of light
That you love to see coming
To bring you closer to things.

Rémige.

Rien que ce mot
Et ce qu'il te rappelle

Devrait suffire
À donner un poème,

Mais tu restes là
À répéter rémige,

À ne pouvoir toucher
Cette plume qui vola,

Avec laquelle
Tu as joué,
Non sans plaindre l'oiseau.

Remex.

Just this word
And what it brings to mind

Should be enough
To give a poem,

But you stay there
Repeating remex,

Unable to touch
That feather that flew away,

With which you've played
Feeling sorry for the bird.

Peupliers alignés
Sur les bords de la route.

Qu'est-ce que cette angoisse
Que vous jetez sur moi ?

Je ne peux rien pour vous
Qu'être pareil à vous.

Poplars aligned
Along the roadside,

What is that anguish
You cast over me?

I can do nothing for you
Except be like you.

Est-ce que je ne vis pas dans un terrier,
Le plus souvent même au fond du terrier ?

Je viens de temps en temps
Au bord du trou
Et regarde ce qu'il y a dehors.

Puis je rentre et je vis
Plus intensément
Ce qui m'a vu.

Je m'offre aussi les nuages
Qui ne m'apportent guère
Pendant le temps où l'on se regarde,

Pas même le désir
De les accompagner.

Am I not living in a burrow,
Most frequently even deep down in a burrow ?

I come out from time to time
To the edge of the hole
And look at what there is outside.

Then I come back
And experience more intensely
That which saw me.

I also treat myself to the clouds
Which hardly give me anything
During the time we look at each other,

Not even the desire
To go along with them.

Tout ce qui dort,
Ce qui ne dort pas.

Ce qui se réveille,
Ce qui s'endort.

Tu inclines à parler
Des choses, des êtres

Comme s'ils étaient
En état de veille,

Acceptaient, ma foi,
De s'entretenir avec toi.

All that sleeps,
All that is not sleeping

All that awakes,
Whatever falls asleep.

You tend to speak
Of things, of beings

As if they were
In a state of wakefulness,

Indeed, were willing
To have a chat with you.

Tous ces frétillements
Que tu sens en toi,
Autour de toi :

Les ramasser,
Les rassembler,
Avant qu'ils ne se perdent,

En faire
Comme une sculpture
Qui défiera le temps.

All this quivering
You feel within you,
Around you:

Collect it,
Assemble it,
Before it gets lost,

Make of it
Something like a sculpture
That will challenge time.

Préférer
Ce qui ne bouge pas
À ce qui bouge.

Et d'abord, ce qui bouge,
On sait ce qu'il peut faire.

Ce qui ne bouge pas
Va peut-être étonner
S'il se met à bouger.

Et puis, ne pas bouger,
C'est bouger autrement :

Bouger dans son intérieur
Sans en avoir l'air,

Mais bouger
Vers quelque chose

Qui ne bouge pas
Ou bouge d'un même mouvement.

Ne pas bouger,
C'est contenir.

Prefer
What doesn't move
To what moves.

For a start, whatever moves,
We know what it can do.

What doesn't move
Will perhaps surprise us
If it starts moving.

And then, not moving,
Moves in a different way:

Moving within oneself
Without showing it,

But moving
Towards something

That does not move
Or moves in the same movement.

Not moving,
Is containing.

Ce n'est pas de marbre que tu rêves
Pour ton poème,

Ni de rien d'aussi dur,
Ni de rien d'aussi froid.

Tu rêverais plutôt
D'un grand bouquet

D'herbes, de feuilles, de pétales
Où l'on pourrait se loger,

N'avoir plus besoin
De regarder ailleurs.

It's not marble you dream of
For your poem.

Nor of anything as hard,
Nor of anything as cold.

Rather you'd dream
Of a huge bunch

Of grasses, leaves and petals
In which you could dwell,

No longer have the need
To look elsewhere.

Sur l'air,
Comme on fait sur une ardoise,

Ecrire des mots
Arrachés aux alentours.

In the air,
As on a slate,

Write words
Wrenched from the surroundings.

Je suis à Paris
Dans mon appartement,
Et la mer me berce.

Je suis allongé dans l'eau,
Je monte et je descends
Avec les vagues,

Je me laisse porter
Par la marée.
Jamais la mer
Ne me manque.

Elle m'accompagne
Dans le poème
Qui se fera peut-être.

I'm in Paris
In my apartment,
And the sea is rocking me.

I lie in the water,
Go up and down
With the waves,

I let myself drift
With the tide.
I never miss
The sea.

It keeps me company
In the poem
I may write.

Dans les brisants,
Dans les cris des goëlands,
Dans l'écume qui retombe en eau,
Dans la marée qui commence à monter,
Dans le goémon qui s'accroche aux rochers,

Je me convie.
Je m'y retrouve.

Into the breakers,
Into the seagulls' cry,
Into the foam that drops back into water,
Into the tide beginning to come in,
Into the seaweed sticking to the rocks,

I invite myself.
I find myself again.

Tu veux sur le papier
Laisser des coquillages,

Différents de couleur,
De forme, de contenu,

Disant l'univers
Comme le solen

Donne la mer.

You want to leave
Shells on the paper,

Different in colour,
Form and content,

Expressing the universe
Just as the razor shell

Gives us the sea.

Je suis allé sur la plage,
J'ai marché le long des vagues.

Je vais et je marche
Pour être compagnon de l'océan,

Avec l'espoir qu'il m'aidera
À trouver comment écrire sur lui.

Et sans doute,
Me connaîtrai-je mieux alors.

I went to the beach,
I walked along by the waves.

I go and walk
To be a companion to the ocean,

With the hope that it will help me
To find how to write about it.

And doubtless
Then I'll know myself better.

Je vois bien que j'existe
Pour l'océan.

Alors, qu'il me traduise
En palourdes, berniques,
En vagues, en rochers,

Je n'en serai pas amoindri,
Bien au contraire.

I can see that I exist
For the ocean.

So let it translate me
Into clams, limpets,
Waves and rocks,

It won't diminish me,
Quite the contrary.

L'océan lui aussi
Ecrit et ne cesse d'écrire.

À chaque marée
Il écrit sur le sable.

Il écrit tous les jours,
Toujours la même chose.

C'est sans doute
Ce qu'il doit se dire,

La même chose, et pourtant
Qui s'en fatigue ?

Ne le jalouse pas :
C'est l'océan.

The ocean also
Writes and never stops.

At each tide
It writes on the sand.

It writes every day,
Always the same thing.

It's probably
What it must say to itself,

The same thing, but then
Who tires of it?

Don't be jealous:
It's the ocean.

Les menhirs de Carnac
Sont autant de poèmes

Que le ciel et le vent
Cherchent à se dédier.

The standing stones of Carnac
Are so many poems

That the sky and the wind
Try to dedicate to each other.

Tous les toits
Te ressemblent.

Toujours ils essayent
De se defendre contre l'espace

Qu'ils tâchent d'épouser
Contre le temps.

All rooftops
Resemble you.

Always they endeavour
To defend themselves against the space

They try to espouse
Against time.

Je me suis abonné
À l'instant

Avec lui je vais
À travers le temps

Qu'il transperce
Pour venir à moi,

Et nous restons ensemble
Comme l'eau et l'étang.

Quand, va savoir pourquoi,
Le contact est rompu,

Je deviens un errant
Ou plutôt

J'ai perdu ce que je suis.

I've taken out a subscription
To the instant

And with it I go
Through the time

It transfixes
To come to me,

And we stay together
Like water and pond.

When, who knows why,
The contact is broken,

I become a wanderer
Or rather

I've lost
What I am.

Quelque chose coule
À travers mon corps

Comme un fleuve
Passe par une écluse,

Quelque chose
D'inattrapable

Et dont j'ignore
S'il me laisse des alluvions.

Ça ne peut pas être
La simple traversée
Par le temps.

Si je dis : c'est la vie,
Cela m'aura rassuré,
Mais je n'aurai rien dit.

Something is running
Through my body

Like a river
Going through sluice gates,

Something
That can't be captured

About which I don't know
Whether it leaves me alluvions.

It can't be
The simple passage
Through time.

If I say: that's life,
It will have reassured me,
But I will have said nothing.

Je veux
Faire de la durée

Mon épouse,
Mon amante.

Avoir avec elle des étreintes
Comme clandestines

Qui me laissent
Epuisé, comblé.

I want
To espouse duration

Make her
My lover.

Hold her in such
Clandestine embraces

As to leave me
Exhausted, fulfilled.

Et si le poème
Était une bougie

Qui se consumerait
Sans jamais s'épuiser ?

What if the poem
Were a candle

That would burn
And never go out?

J'écoute
Et je n'écoute pas.

J'entends
Et je n'entends pas.

Tout se fait sans moi
Et pourtant avec moi

Qui suis ici
Et suis un peu partout,

Entremêlé à tous
Ces destins que j'ignore.

I listen
And do not listen.

I hear
And do not hear.

Everything is done without me
Yet with me

I am here
And I am everywhere,

Mingling with all
Those destinies I know nothing of.

Je voudrais
Parler silence.

Le silence
Parle du centre.

C'est d'eux
Que j'ai besoin.

I would like
To speak silence.

Silence
Speaks of the centre.

They are
What I need.

Cet entrelacs
De pensées, de rêves,
De vues, de visions,
De souvenirs, d'aspirations,

Qui occupe tes loisirs
Et souvent te pèse,

Cet entrelacs,
Le poème l'écarte,
Le chasse
Au profit d'un centre

Où tu trouves l'espace
Pour tes dimensions.

That interlacing
Of thoughts, dreams,
Sights, visions,
Memories, aspirations,

Occupying your leisure
And often a burden to you,

That interlacing,
The poem sets aside,
Sees it off
In favour of a centre

Where you find the space
For your dimensions.

Mais pourquoi, toujours,
Encore écrire ?

Parce que tu sens
Que tu n'es pas
Au centre, dans le noyau ?

But why, always,
Forever write?

Because you feel
That you are not
In the centre, in the nucleus?

Avec des mots
Et leurs souvenirs,

Faire un noyau
Que l'on puisse, ou presque,
Tenir dans la main.

Un noyau de temps.

With words
And their memories,

Make a kernel
One can hold, or almost,
In one's hand,

A kernel of time.

Si je fais couler du sable
De ma main gauche à ma paume droite,

C'est bien sûr pour le plaisir
De toucher la pierre devenue poudre,

Mais c'est aussi et davantage
Pour donner du corps au temps,

Pour ainsi sentir le temps
Couler, s'écouler

Et aussi le faire
Revenir en arrière, se renier.

En faisant glisser du sable,
J'écris un poème contre le temps.

If I pour some sand
From my left hand to my right palm,

It's of course for the pleasure
Of touching powdered stone,

But it's also and more so
To give a body to time,

So as to feel time
Trickling, passing by

And also to make it
Turn back, retract.

By making some sand slip by,
I'm writing a poem against time.

Ce vase blanc
Qui rend le temps plus lent,

Je suis à lui
Plus qu'il n'est à moi.

Il entre, il demeure
Dans mon royaume de jouissance.

This white vase
That makes time slow down,

I belong to it
More than it to me.

It enters into, it remains
In my kingdom of enjoyment.

Il est minuit
Et cela pourrait être
Le centre du poème,

Puisque nous sommes
En plein dans la nuit
Et dans son centre même.

Alors, nous qui cherchons
Toujours à saisir
Quelque chose de plus

Nous pourrions profiter
De ce minuit qui s'offre

Et ne demande
Qu'à s'incarner.

It's midnight
And that might be
The centre of the poem,

Because we are
Fully into night
And in its very centre.

So we who are
Always trying
To grasp something more

We might take advantage
Of midnight's offer

Only asking
To become incarnate.

L'arbre
S'enracine dans la terre.

Le poème s'enracine
Dans ce qu'il devient.

The tree
Is rooted in the earth.

The poem takes root
In what it becomes.

Que pèse
Un hectare de plaine ?

Il pèse pour toi
Tout ce qui maintenant
Est venu de lui dans le poème.

What does
An hectare of plain weigh?

For you it weighs
Whatever of itself has now come
Into the poem.

Tu ne te situes pas
Au niveau de l'azur.

Plutôt avec
Les colza—et les comme toi.

You do not situate yourself
On the level of the azure sky.

But rather with
The colza plants—and others like you.

Si la pervenche—

Si le ciel—

Si la source—

Si l'arbre—

Si la pierre—

Si le lac—

Si les ongles—

Si—

Et tu es toujours
Partie prenante.

If the periwinkle—

If the sky—

If the spring—

If the tree—

If the stone—

If the lake—

If the fingernails—

If—

And you are still
Involved.

Je ne suis pas bison
Et je me sens ruminant.

Je ne suis pas goéland
Et je me sens voler.

Je ne suis pas charbon
Et je me sens brûler.

Je ne suis pas caillou
Et je me sens durer.

Je ne suis pas pourceau
Et je me sens grogner.

Je ne suis pas Pégase
Et je me sens errer.

Je ne suis pas cravache
Et je me sens frapper.

Je ne suis pas écolier
Et je me sens apprendre.

Je ne suis pas archer
Et je me sens tirer.

Je ne suis pas prélat
Et je me sens bénir.

Je ne suis pas gardien
Et je me sens veiller.

I am not a bison
And I feel like a ruminant.

I am not a seagull
And I feel myself flying

I am not coal
And I feel myself burning.

I am not a pebble
And I feel myself lasting.

I am not a piglet
And I feel myself grunting.

I am not Pegasus
And I feel myself wandering.

I am not a riding-stock
And I feel myself hitting.

I am not a schoolboy
And I feel I am learning.

I am not an archer
And I feel myself shooting.

I am not a prelate
And I feel myself blessing.

I am not a guard
And I feel myself keeping watch.

Je suis un ruminant.
Je broute des mots.

I am a ruminant
I graze on words.

Qui a le gouvernement
Quand tu écris le poème ?

Tu le partages
Avec bien plus fort que toi.

Après, tu joueras le rôle
Du Conseil d'État.

Who governs
When you write the poem?

You share it
With a higher power than yourself.

Afterwards you will play the part
Of Council of State.

Le rire est bon.

Pour certains le rire
S'arrête aux frontières du poème
Comme à des murailles.

Laughter is good.

For some, laughter
Stops at the frontiers of the poem
As at city walls.

Lors de la quête
Acharnée du poème

Tu as quelque chose
De l'escargot
Après la pluie.

During the relentless
Quest for the poem

You have something about you
Of the snail
After the rain.

Bien qu'abîmé
Par un long usage,

Et qu'il soit de ces termes
Que l'on nomme poétiques,

Je me sers
Du mot azur, je l'écris,

Parce qu'il dit
Le ciel bleu, de ce bleu

Inviolé
Même par le firmament.

In spite of wear and tear
Through long use,

And it's one of those terms
Called poetic,

I use
The word azure, I write it,

For it expresses
The blue sky, of a blue

Inviolate
Even by the firmament.

Depuis quelques jours
Et presqu'en permanence
Il y a devant moi,

Que mes yeux soient ouverts
Ou qu'ils soient fermés,

Une équerre
Peut-être bien de bois,

Un peu plus grande
Qu'une figure humaine,

Et l'équerre se tient
Verticale au-dessus d'une eau

Tout comme elle muette
Voulant dire elle aussi
J'aimerais savoir quoi.

For several days
Almost all the time
There is before me,

Whether my eyes are open
Or whether they are closed,

A geometry triangle
A wooden one perhaps,

Somewhat larger
Than a human figure,

And the triangle is poised
Vertically above water

Silent like itself,
Wanting to say also
I wonder what.

Toujours aux aguets
Quoi que je fasse,

Désirant
Je ne sais quoi.

Je ne l'apprendrai
Que lorsque cette espèce de chose

Je l'aurai là,
Dans mes filets -

Quels filets ?

Always watching like a hawk
Whatever I do,

Wanting
I know not what.

I'll not find out
Until whatever it is

I have it here,
In my nets -

What nets?

Tant de choses
Dans le monde.

Ton envie
De tout posséder.

Alors tu prends
Une chose ou plusieurs,

Tu ne les choisis pas
Mais elles s'imposent,

Et parfois ça te réussit :
Ces choses
Te qualifient le monde.

So many things
In the world.

Your desire
To possess everything.

So you take
One thing or several,

You don't choose them
But they intrude

And sometimes that suits you
These things
Describe the world for you.

Je vois passer les nuages
Et l'envie me prend pour une fois
De les accompagner.

Je monte vers eux
Et je vais avec eux
Longtemps.

Je ne vois pas beaucoup les alentours,
Je regarde surtout en eux
Et c'est pourquoi

Je ne trouve à dire
Que l'extase.

I can see clouds passing by
And for once I feel
Like going with them.

I go up to them
And I go with them
For a long time.

I don't see the surroundings much,
I look mostly into them
And that's why

I can only express
Ecstasy.

Laissez-moi m'enfoncer
Dans ma mer imaginaire
Et pourtant vraie.

Let me go deep
Into my imaginary
Yet real sea.

Faire
Que se trouver au bord

Ce soit
Plonger dedans.

Make it happen
That being on the edge

Is
Plunging in.

Tu sais qu'en écrivant
Tu vas apprendre.

Si tu croyais ne rien apprendre
Tu n'écrirais pas.

Chaque fois
Tu sais que tu vas saisir
Un embryon de définitif.

Tu ressembles
Au pêcheur qui attend

De tenir bientôt
Du vivant.

You know that by writing
You're going to learn.

If you thought you wouldn't learn anything
You wouldn't write.

Each time
You know you'll grasp
An embryo of the definitive.

You are like
The fisherman waiting

Soon to catch
Something alive.

Si tu écris,
C'est aussi pour te protéger—

De quoi ?

De quoi as-tu peur
Quand tu n'as pas peur ?

If you write,
It is also to protect yourself—

From what?

What are you afraid of
When you're not afraid?

Je sais
Que tu es un arbre.

Toi tu sais
Que tu es toi.

Ferme en toi,
Rayonnant.

Ne me repousse pas.

I know
That you're a tree.

You know
That you're you,

Firm in yourself,
Radiant.

Don't push me away.

Ce passereau
Sur la branche de l'acacia

Est aussi
À la recherche de son poème.

—Il n'a pas dû le trouver,
Il est parti.

This sparrow
On the branch of the acacia

Is also
Looking for its poem.

—It can't have found it,
It's gone.

Je n'écris pas de toi,
Je n'écris pas de nous
Quand je te vis le plus.

Rien n'est alors
Que de nous vivre,

Quand tellement je suis à toi
Que je suis plus toi que moi.

J'écris plutôt de toi
Afin de revivre ces temps

Restés en moi, mûrs du besoin
De les dépasser

Vers le plus
Qu'on peut supporter.

I don't write about you,
I don't write about us
When I live you most.

Then nothing exists
But living ourselves,

When I am so much yours
That I am more you than me.

I write rather about you
So as to relive those times

That stay within me, ripe with the need
To go beyond them

Towards the most
That can be borne.

Ces moments

Où voir une mouche,
Voir un liseron,

Voir la cour après
Le coucher du soleil,

Voir sa propre main,
Voir bouger sa jambe,

Ne rien voir—

Et c'est la plénitude.

Those moments

When to see a fly,
To see a convolvulus,

To see the courtyard
After sunset,

To see one's own hand,
To see one's leg move,

To see nothing—

And that is plenitude.

C'est plus souvent
Un filet qu'un torrent.

Tu forces quelque peu
Le courant à passer.

Parfois il s'emballe,
Tu as peine à suivre

Mais tu sais recueillir,
Tu es là

Pour l'arrivée,
Si elle a lieu.

It's more often
A trickle than a torrent.

You barely force
The current to pass.

At times, it rushes,
You find it hard to follow

But you know how to collect it,
You're there

For the arrival,
If it takes place.

Je suspends mon heur
Au poème.

Comme l'araignée
S'accroche à son fil.

I hang my fortune
On the poem

Just as the spider
Hooks onto its thread.

Le poème
Ne tue pas le vide,
Il l'éloigne.

La poème fait toucher
Le vide
Qui le borde.

Ce vide plus fort,
Plus dominateur
Que lui.

Si bien
Que c'est sa présence
À la lisière

Qui donne sa puissance
Au poème
Dans ses limites.

The poem
Doesn't kill the void,
It moves it away.

The poem lets us touch
The void
Surrounding it.

That void stronger,
More dominating
Than itself.

So that
It is its presence
At the edge

That gives its strength
To the poem
Within its limits.

Faire en moi cette vacance
Qui demande
À être vaincu.

Cerner davantage en moi
Ce presque puits
Qui fait malaise.

M'apprendre
À découvrir un creux si fort
Qu'il appelle

Cette autre chose
Dont les mots deviendront
Les chargés du pouvoir.

Make within myself that emptiness
That demands
To be vanquished.

Encompass within myself
That almost wellshaft
That forms disquiet.

Teach myself
To discover so compelling a chasm
That it calls out to

This other thing
Whose words will become
Executives of power.

En toi cette force—
Comme si
Tu ne savais rien—

Et qui fait.

In you this strength—
As if
You knew nothing—

And which acts.

Pire que tout :
La présence du rien.

Tu le sens
Tu le portes.

Worse than anything:
The presence of nothingness.

You feel it,
You bear it.

Tu n'imites pas
Le rossignol.

Tu l'accueilles,
Tu le vénères.

Tu laisses germer en toi
Ce qu'il y sème

Du jour, du soir,
De ce qui fait vibrer l'horizon.

You don't imitate
The nightingale.

You welcome it,
You venerate it.

You let germinate within you
What it sows there

Of the day, of the evening,
Of what makes the horizon vibrate.

Attends. Continue
À résister.

La pression n'est pas
Tout à fait assez forte.

N'écris pas maintenant,
Pas tout de suite.

Tu peux encore
Tenir.

Wait. Carry on
Resisting.

The pressure is not
Quite strong enough.

Don't write just now,
Not straight away.

You can still
Hold fast.

Supporter son corps
N'est pas toujours commode.

Quand tu écris
C'est comme s'il n'existait pas.

S'il se fondait
Dans plus vaste que lui.

Coping with one's body
Is not always easy.

When you write
It's as if it didn't exist,

As if it melted
Into something greater than itself.

Inextricable,
Ce dans quoi tu vis :

Un dédale, un mélange
De tout et de rien.

Alors tu te rabats
Sur l'élémentaire,

Tout ce qui fut
À l'origine
Et qui demeure.

Là, tu peux t'appuyer
Sur ce qui te ressemble.

Inextricable,
What you are living in:

A labyrinth, a mixture
Of all and nothing.

So you fall back on
Basic things,

All that was
In the beginning
And still remains.

There, you can lean
On what resembles you.

N'attends pas plus longtemps.

Si tu ne saisis pas le poème
Aussitôt qu'il exige,

Peut-être jamais plus
Il ne reviendra.

Peut-être
Il se détruira

Ou s'engouffrera dans un monde,
À combien de dimensions ?

Wait no longer.

If you do not take hold of the poem
As soon as it demands,

Maybe it will never
Ever come back.

Maybe
It will destroy itself

Or become engulfed in a world,
Of how many dimensions?

Écrire le poème
C'est d'ici se donner un ailleurs
Plus ici qu'auparavant.

Writing the poem
Is from here to give oneself an elsewhere
More here than before.

Le poème
Te sort du complot du poids et du temps
Pendant qu'en lui tu plonges.

Tu es comme la vapeur
Qui redevient eau,
Se refait vapeur.

The poem
Brings you out of the plot between weight and time
While you plunge into it.

You are like steam
That becomes water,
And goes back to steam.

Être
À longueur de temps

Un poème
Exponentiel.

To be
All life long

An exponential
Poem.

Le poème :

Un contenant
Qui trouve sa forme

Au fur et au mesure
Qu'il se remplit.

The poem:

A container
Finding its form

As little by little
It is filled.

La nuit accouche des étoiles,
Toi, tu accouches des poèmes :

Lentement,
En tâtonnant.

Mais la nuit
A plus de talent.

Night gives birth to stars,
You give birth to poems:

Slowly,
Feeling your way.

But night
Has more talent.

Tu voudrais bien écrire
Autrement.

Voir naître sous ta main,
Sous tes yeux,

Quelque forme
Qui ne te rappelle rien,

Mais c'est en vain :
Tu es condamné.

You'd like to write
Differently.

To see some form
That reminds you of nothing

Come to life in your hands
In your eyes,

But it's in vain:
You're condemned.

Est-ce que je vois
Ce que je vois ?

Est-ce que j'entends
Ce que j'entends ?

Je vois peut-être
Ce que j'entends,

J'entends peut-être
Ce que je vois.

Peut-être rien
De tout cela,

Un souffle de sons,
De couleurs, de formes.

Do I see
What I see?

Do I hear
What I hear?

Maybe I see
What I hear,

Maybe I hear
What I see.

Maybe nothing
Of all that,

A wisp of sounds,
Colours, forms.

Au-dessus de toutes ces misères
Que tu côtoies, traverses,
Il y a un espace.

L'étonnant
C'est que tu n'arrives
À cet espace
Qu'avec des mots

Que tu manies
Comme l'oiseau
Avec des brindilles
Se construit un nid.

Way above all this discomfort
That you come across, experience,
There's a space.

The surprising thing
Is that you only reach
This space
With words

That you handle
The way a bird
Out of twigs
Builds a nest.

Pas vu
La couleur de l'arbre
Ne même sa forme.

Je vivais trop en lui
Son épopée
Au soleil couchant.

Didn't see
The colour of the tree
Or even its shape.

Within it I was living too intensely
Its epic
In the sunset.

J'ai envie
D'une chevauchée

À travers
Je ne sais quel espace,

Sur des vers
Qu'il me faut inventer.

I feel like
Riding

Across
I know not what space,

On lines of poetry
I have to invent.

Le poème est là

Où celui qui s'y love
En arrive presque

À toucher l'espace.

The poem is where

Whoever curls up in it
Almost manages

To touch space.

Dans le poème on ne peut pas
S'asseoir à l'aise.

Il vous faut tenir debout,
Monter rayonnant.

Le monde vous entoure de près
Tout en devenant moins lourd,
Traversé par une lumière
Qui ne vient pas d'ailleurs.

—Vous êtes poursuivi.

In the poem you can't
Sit comfortably.

You have to stand up straight,
Rise up radiant.

The world surrounds you closely
Becoming less heavy,
Penetrated by a light
Not coming from elsewhere.

—You're being followed.

Fatalement, rimer
C'est répéter, piétiner,

Poser un son
Pour le retrouver.

Or, je veux que les mots
Aillent à l'aventure,

Et que l'on découvre
S'ils s'accordent,

Pourquoi faut-il, d'ailleurs,
Qu'ils s'accordent ?

Inevitably, rhyming
Is repeating, shuffling,

Placing a sound
To find it again.

But I want words
To be adventurous,

So that we discover
Whether they agree.

But why
Should they agree?

Pourquoi te crois-tu
Responsable à perpétuité ?

Parce que tu parles
De tout et même

De ce qui ne va pas
Jusqu'à prendre corps ?

Why do you think you're
Forever responsible?

Because you speak
About everything and even

About what's not likely
To materialize ?

C'était une pierre.

Ce n'était pas une voix
Qui venait de loin,
Des profondeurs de l'air,
De la nuit.

Ce n'était qu'une pierre
Qui près de toi
Ronronnait son mal -

Ou le tien.

It was a stone.

It wasn't a voice
Coming from afar,
From deep in the air,
The night.

It was only a stone
That close to you
Was purring away its pain

Or your own.

Ce soleil dans le ciel
C'est toi qui l'as plaqué
Au dessus de l'horizon.

Tu l'as inventé
Tu l'as projeté
Tu le nourris.

Il t'éclaire,
Il te chauffe.

La journée
Sera bonne.

This sun in the sky,
It's you who put it there
Above the horizon.

You invented it,
You planned it;
You nourished it.

It gives you light,
It warms you.

The day
Will be good.

Ce que le poème
Finit par accrocher,
Incorporer

Dans son univers
Sans dimension.

What the poem
Succeeds in
Incorporating

In its immeasurable
Universe.

Je ne demande qu'à rester
À cet endroit où je me trouve.

Je cherche à le posséder

Dans son tout et dans ses détails
Jusqu'à me confondre avec lui

Ou mieux, le confondre avec moi.

All I ask is to stay
In this place where I am

I'm trying to make it mine

In its entirety and its details
Until I'm mingled with it

Or, better, mingle it with me.

Il n'y a pas que la mémoire.

Il y a ces réminiscences
De ce que l'on n'a pas vécu,
Qui nous viennent d'on ne sait où:

Aujourd'hui, c'est l'oeil du requin,
C'est la myopie de l'horizon.

There is not only memory.

There are reminiscences
Of what we have not lived
That come from who knows where:

Today it's the eye of the shark,
The short-sightedness of the horizon.

Le poème
Se fait chalut

Dans lequel se prend
On ne sait quoi,

Qui n'existe pas
En dehors de lui

Et qui restera
Vivant en lui,

À la fois vibrant
Et figé.

The poem
Becomes a trawler

In which we catch
Who knows what,

That doesn't exist
Outside of it

And will remain
Alive within it,

At once vibrant
And still.

Un travail : créer
De la tension
Entre les mots,

Faire que chacun
En appelle un
Ou plusieurs autres.

Ils ne tiennent
Pas tellement à venir
De leur plein gré.

Quand ils arrivent
Ils sont arrimés
Irrévocablement

Par un silence
Qui ne sera
Jamais rompu.

A task: to create
Tension
Between words,

Make each one
Appeal to one
Or several others.

They're not
Particularly eager
To come willingly.

When they come
They are stowed away
Irrevocably

By a silence
Which will never
Be broken.

Que faire
Dans une ville
Inconnue, désertique

Qui vous a de beautés anciennes
Presque assommé,

Et qui vous laisse en dehors d'elle
Dans la chambre anonyme
D'un très moderne hotel ?

Tenter
Le dedans du poème ?

What can one do
In an unfamiliar,
Desert town

Which has almost bowled you over
With ancient beauty,

And which leaves you outside of it
In the anonymous room
Of a very modern hotel?

Try
The inside of the poem?

Si tu cèdais,

Tu en reviendrais
Toujours à l'armoire,
À son chêne et –

Ne recommence pas.

If you gave in,

You would always
Come back to the *armoire*,
To its oak and—

Don't start again.

Vous êtes seul.
On connaît ça.

Mitraillez
L'entourage du monde entier
Avec des mots,

Les vôtres, bien sûr,
Ceux qui vous mitraillent
À l'interieur.

Essayez !
Vos mots, il se peut

Qu'ils vous reviennent,
Habités,

Tout prêts
À vous occuper.

You're on your own.
It's a known fact.

Bombard
The surroundings and the whole world
With words.

Your own, of course,
Those that bombard you
On the inside.

Try!
Maybe your words

Will come back to you,
Inhabited,

Ready
To occupy you.

Je n'en pouvais plus
D'entendre ce morceau de granit

Me raconter son histoire
Depuis les origines.

J'avais beau lui dire : je sais,
Le morceau de granit continuait :

Soleil, déluge, incendie, ténèbres
Et le pire : l'eau goutte à goutte
Pendant des millénaires.

I'd had enough
Of hearing this piece of granite

Telling me its story
From the beginning of time.

Even when I said : I know,
The piece of granite would go on:

Sun, flood, fire, darkness
And worst of all : water falling drop by drop
For thousands of years.

L'humilité te sied.
Elle t'est pour ainsi dire
Fonctionnelle.

Tu avances
À travers un magma
À la façon d'un rat,

Mais lui est sûr
De son itinéraire

Et quand il grignote,
Il sait dans quoi.

Humility suits you.
It is so to speak
Functional.

You advance
Across magma
The way a rat does,

But it is certain
Of its itinerary

And when it nibbles
It knows on what.

Le mot du poème

Connaît le malaise,
Le besoin de posséder,

Celui de savoir
Où sont ses limites

Et s'il peut brûler
Sans se détruire.

The word of the poem

Knows the unease,
The need to possess itself,

The need to know
Where its limits are

And if it can burn
Without being destroyed.

On dit. En fait,
On ne dit pas,

Mais c'est
Comme si.

Quelque chose passe
À travers le dire,
Cet effort pour dire.

La preuve :
D'autres le répètent,
Et ça les aide.

People say. In fact,
People don't,
But it's
As if.

Something passes
Through speech,
This effort to speak.

The proof:
Others repeat it,
And that helps them.

Je vous donnerai des poèmes
Où vous vivrez

Comme l'olivier
Vit dans sa terre.

Vous y gagnerez
De faire vous aussi
Vos olives.

I will give you poems
In which you will live

Just as the olive tree
Lives in its earth.

It will be to your advantage
If you too
Do your olives.

Quoi que tu fasses
Le poème
Garde mystère.

Pas plus
Que l'arbre et le buisson,

Que la palourde
Et sa coquille,

Que ta bague
De quartz rutile.

Whatever you do
The poem
Holds mystery.

No more
Than the tree and the bush,

Than the clam
And its shell,

Than your ring
Of rutile quartz.

Qui te dira
Si ton poème
Est poème ?

S'il restera gravé
Dans l'espace durable
Où se tient le poème ?

Who'll tell you
Whether your poem
Is a poem?

Whether it will remain engraved
In enduring space
Where the poem has its place?

Le poème
Nous met au monde.

The poem
Brings us into the world.

J'ai été obligé
De longer le mur.

Je croyais folâtrer,
Mais j'étais
Le féal du poème.

I was obliged
To stay close to the wall.

I thought my behaviour was a courtier's
But I was
The vassal of the poem.

Quand aurai-je
Pour de bon

Parlé à la table,
Parlé de la table,

Afin qu'elle cesse
De m'interroger,

De me demander
De lui parler d'elle.

When shall I,
For good,

Have spoken to the table,
Have spoken about the table,

So that it stops
Questioning me,

Asking me
To talk about it?

Forcé d'écrire ?
Je n'en ai pas envie.

J'aimerais
Rester là, immobile,

À regarder le ciel,
Il n'y a pas plus bleu,

Et de temps en temps
L'horizon et ses approches.

Je voudrais
Me passer des mots.

Forced to write?
I don't feel like it.

I'd like
To stay here, without moving,

Looking at
The exceptionally blue sky,

And from time to time
The horizon and its vicinity.

I'd like
To manage without words.

Je ne sais pas
Si je serai compris,

Je ne sais même pas
Si je me comprendrai.

Je continue
À soupeser la pomme.

I don't know
Whether I'll be understood,

I don't even know
Whether I'll understand myself.

I carry on
Weighing up the apple.

Pénible d'éprouver
Qu'on n'a presque rien révélé

De ce qu'on porte
Et qui vient de ce monde
Inentamé, si lourd,

Toujours plein de ces choses
Qui serinent
Qu'on les délivre.

Painful to experience
That one has revealed hardly anything

About what one bears
And which comes from this world
Intact, so heavy.

Always full of those things
That drum it into us
That we are to release them.

Aller
Dans le règne
Où faire mes découvertes.

Pourquoi règne ?
Je ne vois pas
Qui régnerait

Dans ces zones
Où je m'enfonce
Tant que je peux.

Go
Into the kingdom
To make my discoveries.

Why kingdom?
I can't see
Who would reign

In those zones
Into which I go
As far as I can.

Ne me demandez pas
Comment j'arrive.

Je n'en sais rien
Moi-même,

Je viens du pays noir
Où se forment les sources.

Don't ask me
How I manage.

I know nothing about it
Myself.

I come from the dark country
Where springwaters are formed.

C'est parce qu'il existe
Tout cela qui n'apparaît pas

Qui a force,
Impact,

Et qui pour de vrai
Régit le monde,

C'est cause de ce vague,
À cause de ta peur

Que tellement tu t'intéresses,
T'accroches

À ce que l'on peut toucher,
Ce sur quoi appuyer la joue.

It's because of the existence
Of everything that is not apparent

Which has strength,
Impact,

And which for ever
Governs the world,

It's because of this vagueness,
Because of your fear

That you are so interested,
So hooked onto

What can be touched,
What you can press your cheek to.

Si tu t'aimais

Comme tu aimes
Le poème que tu cherches,

Peut-être
Tu n'écrirais plus.

If you loved yourself

As you love
The poem you are looking for,

Perhaps
You would write no longer.

Tu sais
Qu'il n'y a pas,

Qu'il n'y aura jamais,
Au plein de tes jours,

L'arrivée,

La vraie,
La définitive –

Et pourtant tu fais comme si.

You know
That there is not,

That there will never be,
For as long as you live,

The true,
The definitive

Arrival,

However
You act as if there would.

La beauté doit venir
D'un autre monde

Qui s'avance
Jusqu'au nôtre

Et parfois même
L'enveloppe.

Regarde
Cette chapelle romane,

Les prés alentour,
Le ciel qui s'incline,

Regarde et maintenant
Ose dire où nous sommes.

Beauty must come
From another world

Which makes its way
To ours

And sometimes even
Covers it.

Look
At this romanesque chapel,

The meadows around it,
The sky bending over,

Look and now
Dare to say where we are.

Rêvé
D'un seul poème

Qui dirait la somme
De tes rapports avec le monde
Et ce toi-même en toi.

La somme que le tout
Doit dire à travers toi.

Dreamt
Of a single poem

That would express the whole
Of your relationship with the world
And that self within you.

Everything that it all
Must say through you.

Nous aussi
Nous sommes des volcans,

Mais eux, ils peuvent –
Impunément.

We too
Are volcanoes,

But they can be so—
With impunity

La musique entraîne.
Toi, tu ne veux pas être entraîné
Pas maintenant.

Il faut rester ici
À regarder autour de toi.

Regarde, regarde
Et parle

À tout ce qui t'entoure,
Se tait et te défie.

Music carries you away.
You don't want to be carried away.
Not now.

You must stay here
Look around you.

Look, look
And talk

To everything around you,
That is silent and resists you.

Vais-je
M'approcher ?

Arbre, rocher, talus,
Je vous connais.

La distance
Ne m'empêche pas

De vous parler,
De vous écouter,

Mais vous toucher
Me ferait du bien.

Shall I
Come close?

Tree, rock, slope,
I know you.

Distance
Doesn't stop me

From talking to you,
From hearing you,

But to touch you
Would do me good.

La surface est là
Pour qu'on la traverse—

La traverse vers quoi ?
On ne le sait pas.

Une fois la surface traversée,
On se vivra

Épousant un intérieur
Autre que soi-même.

The surface is there
To be crossed—

Cross it where to?
We don't know.

Once the surface is crossed,
We can live our lives

Espousing an interior
Other than ourselves.

Être relié
À l'immémorial,

Planer à travers les temps,
Qu'ils soient de misère

Où d'éblouissement.

To be linked,
To the immemorial,

To soar above the times,
Be they dark

Or dazzling.

Il n'y aura pas
De soleil dans la nuit,
Mais il y a son souvenir

Et le frémissement
Que donne la rencontre

Entre ce souvenir
Et le prochain retour de la clarté.

There will be
No sun in the night,
But there is its memory

And the thrill
Of the encounter

Between this memory
And the imminent return of daylight.

Ce qui tout à l'heure
Était dans l'eau,
Qui ne s'y reflète plus :

Une marche, un défilé rocheux,
Une ébauche de machinerie,
Un crayon en train d'écrire

Et le regard, ce regard
Qui n'était pas pour toi,

Qui a disparu
Comme le reste,
Sans doute en même temps,

Vers le même néant –
Ou vers quoi ?

What was in the water
Earlier on,
Which is no longer reflected in it:

A step, a narrow rocky pass,
An engine room project,
A pencil writing

And the look, that look
Which was not for you,

Which has disappeared,
Like the rest,
Probably at the same time,

Towards the same nothingness—
Or towards what?

Les débauches d'aurore
S'épuiseront avant
Que tu ne sois maître de l'aube –

Et tu resteras là
Devant un jour naissant

Pas plus ni moins
Miraculeux qu'un autre,

Où tu attendras
Ce que tu attends
À tout moment,

Pour supporter
L'insupportable,
En faire quelque chose.

Daybreak's debauchery
Will come to an end
Before you're the master of dawn -

And you'll stay here
With a new-born day

Neither more nor less
Miraculous than another,

Where you'll await
What you wait for
Each moment,

To bear
The unbearable,
To do something with it

Je n'irai pas
À la recherche d'un paysage
Pour le découvrir ou le revoir.

J'irai là
Où les hasards, la nécessité
M'amèneront,

Et parfois je rencontrerai un lieu
Où avoir envie de rester
Le temps de l'oublier

Pour un lui-même
Encore plus cher à qui
Ne demande rien.

I'll not go out
Looking for a landscape
To discover it or see it again.

I'll go
Wherever danger and need
Will take me,

And sometimes I'll find a place
Where I feel like staying
Until I forget it

For a self
Even dearer to someone
Who asks for nothing.

Un programme
Pour aujourd'hui :

Tu es fleur
Et tu vois
Entrer l'abeille.

A programme
For today:

You are a flower
And you see
The bee going in.

J'ai bien cru
Que cette violette
M'a souri.

Elle a dû se rappeler
Comment j'ai vécu avec elle
Dans l'une ou l'autre
De mes insomnies.

I really thought
That violet
Smiled at me.

It must have remembered
How I lived with it
In one or other
Of my insomnias.

Être
Où et quoi ?

N'importe où,
Mais pas rien qu'en soi.

Être dans le monde.
Fragment, élément du monde.

Supérieur à rien,
Pas à quiconque, pas à la pluie qui tombe,

Se sentir égal
Et pareil au pissenlit, à la limace,

Inférieur à rien,
Ni au baobab, ni à l'horizon,

Vivre avec tout
Ce qui est en dehors et en dedans,

Tout ce qui est au monde,
Dans le monde,

Fétu de paille, non !
Cathédrale, non !

Un souffle
Qui essaie de durer.

To be
Where and what?

No matter where,
But not only in oneself.

To be in the world.
A fragment, an element of the world.

Superior to nothing,
To nobody, not even to the falling rain,

To feel the equal
And the same as the dandelion, the slug,

Inferior to nothing,
Neither the baobab, nor the horizon,

To live with all
That is outside and inside,

Everything of the world,
In the world.

Wisp of straw, no!
Cathedral, no!

A breath of life
Trying to last.

Tu ne seras pas la rose,
Elle ne sera pas toi,

Mais entrer vous il y a
Ce qui vous est commun,

Que vous savez vivre
Et faire partager.

You'll not be the rose,
It won't be you,

But between you there is
What you have in common,

Knowing how to live
And knowing how to share.

September 1985–March 1988

Maureen Smith lives in France where, as Professor of English and American Literature, she taught in universities in Paris and Angers until her retirement in 2002. Trilingual, she specialized in contemporary poetry, and has written articles in English, French and Spanish on contemporary writers and painters. Her book on Denise Levertov, Denise Levertov, *le don de poésie*, was published in Paris, and her translation of Guillevic's *Vivre en poésie/Living in Poetry* in Dublin. She is involved in the Anglo-French Poetry Festival, and writes in its magazine *La Traductière*.

WWW.BLACKWIDOWPRESS.COM

This book was set in Simoncini Garamond. The titling font is Aculida, a modernistic typeface used by many of the Dadaists in their typographic artworks.

typeset & designed by Windhaven Press
www.windhaven.com

TITLES FROM BLACK WIDOW PRESS

TRANSLATION SERIES

Chanson Dada: Selected Poems by Tristan Tzara
Translated with an introduction and essay by Lee Harwood.

Approximate Man and Other Writings by Tristan Tzara
Translated and edited by Mary Ann Caws.

Poems of André Breton: A Bilingual Anthology
Translated with essays by Jean-Pierre Cauvin and Mary Ann Caws.

Last Love Poems of Paul Eluard
Translated with an introduction by Marilyn Kallet.

Capital of Pain by Paul Eluard
Translated by Mary Ann Caws, Patricia Terry, and Nancy Kline.

Love, Poetry (L'amour la poésie) by Paul Eluard
Translated with an essay by Stuart Kendall.

The Sea and Other Poems by Guillevic
Translated by Patricia Terry. Introduction by Monique Chefdor.

Essential Poems and Writings of Robert Desnos: A Bilingual Anthology
Edited with an introduction and essay by Mary Ann Caws.

Essential Poems and Writings of Joyce Mansour: A Bilingual Anthology
Translated with an introduction by Serge Gavronsky.

Poems of A.O. Barnabooth by Valery Larbaud
Translated by Ron Padgett and Bill Zavatsky.

EyeSeas (Les Ziaux) by Raymond Queneau
Translated with an introduction by Daniela Hurezanu and Stephen Kessler.

To Speak, to Tell You? by Sabine Sicaud
Translated by Norman R. Shapiro. Introduction & notes by Odile Ayral-Clause.

Art Poétique by Guillevic
Translated by Maureen Smith.

Furor and Mystery and Other Writings by René Char (Forthcoming)
Edited and translated by Mary Ann Caws and Nancy Kline.

La Fontaine's Bawdy by Jean de la Fontaine (Forthcoming)
Translated with an introduction by Norman R. Shapiro.

Inventor of Love & Other Writings by Ghérasim Luca (Forthcoming)
Translated by Julian and Laura Semilian. Introduction by Andrei Codrescu.
Essay by Petre Răileanu.

The Big Game by Benjamin Péret (Forthcoming)
Translated with an introduction by Marilyn Kallet.

I Want No Part in It and Other Writings by Benjamin Péret (Forthcoming)
Translated with an introduction by James Brook.

Essential Poems and Writings of Jules Laforgue (Forthcoming)
Translated and edited by Patricia Terry.

Preversities: A Jacques Prévert Sampler (Forthcoming)
Translated and edited by Norman R. Shapiro.

MODERN POETRY SERIES

An Alchemist with One Eye on Fire by Clayton Eshleman

Archaic Design by Clayton Eshleman

Backscatter: New and Selected Poems by John Olson

Crusader-Woman by Ruxandra Cesereanu
Translated by Adam J. Sorkin. Introduction by Andrei Codrescu.

The Grindstone of Rapport: A Clayton Eshleman Reader
Forty years of poetry, prose, and translations by Clayton Eshleman.

Packing Light: New and Selected Poems by Marilyn Kallet

Forgiven Submarine by Ruxandra Cesereanu and Andrei Codrescu

The Caveat Onus by Dave Brinks (Forthcoming)
The complete cycle, four volumes combined.

Fire Exit by Robert Kelly (Forthcoming)

NEW POETS SERIES

Signal from Draco: New and Selected Poems by Mebane Robertson

LITERARY THEORY/BIOGRAPHY SERIES

Revolution of the Mind: The Life of André Breton by Mark Polizzotti
(Forthcoming)
Revised and augmented edition.

www.blackwidowpress.com